LEGACY OF POETRY

A Gift from the Heart

By
Flora Sanders

PublishAmerica
Baltimore

© 2010 by Flora Sanders.
All rights reserved. No part of this book may be reproduced, stored in a retrieval system or transmitted in any form or by any means without the prior written permission of the publishers, except by a reviewer who may quote brief passages in a review to be printed in a newspaper, magazine or journal.

First printing

PublishAmerica has allowed this work to remain exactly as the author intended, verbatim, without editorial input.

Hardcover: 978-1-4489-5776-7
Softcover: 978-1-4489-8984-3
PUBLISHED BY PUBLISHAMERICA, LLLP
www.publishamerica.com
Baltimore

Printed in the United States of America

Table of Contents

SIGNS OF FAITH
WHEN I PRAY 13
BUT… 15
DOWN AT THE WELL 17
HOW MUCH? 19
I, EVE 20
I GIVE YOU MY ALL 22
MASTERPIECE 23
THE BURDENS 25
UPON MOUNT CALVARY 27
SOME DAYS, LORD 29
ALL THAT MATTERS 30
HEAVEN SENT 31
SANCTUARY 33
LAMENTATION 34
CHAINS THAT BIND 36
DAUGHTERS EMPOWERED TO POSSESS
    THE PROMISE 38
THE LOVE I OWE 39
SON SHINE 40
MORNING JOY 41
ENDLESS TALK 42
REFINING FIRE 43
GLITTERING HOPE 45
HE WAS ALWAYS THERE 47

PRAISE!	48
IF…	49
GO TELL THEM	50
IT'S ABOUT MY SAVIOR	51
GUIDE MY STEPS	53
I AM A SERVANT	54
HEART OF GRATITUDE	56
THE VISITOR	57

SIGHTS AND SOUNDS OF LIFE

THY MOST EXCELLENT HANDIWORK	61
MY HEART'S SONG	63
ALL IN A DAY'S WORK	64
I AM HIS WOMAN	66
OLD MAN WINTER	68
AN EARLY SPRING	69
ANOTHER EASTER SUNDAY MORNING	71
THE SUMMERS OF OUR YOUTH	72

SPECIAL PEOPLE

BELOVED	77
THE CALLING	78
TRIBUTE TO A SPECIAL LADY	80
A RARE JEWEL	82
TO MY SISTER	84
SISTERS IN CHRIST	86
CICILY EVANGELINE	88
JOSEPH ZACHARIA	90
THAT'S WHY I CALL YOU FRIEND	92
TRUE FRIENDSHIPS	93
STEPPING OUT	94
WHAT IS A NEIGHBOR?	95
ONE MAN STANDS UP	96

MEMORABLE TIMES AND EVENTS
AN ATTITUDE OF THANKSGIVING 99
ONE HOLY NIGHT IN BETHLEHEM 101
GLAD TIDINGS 104
WHILE ON THE CROSS THAT DAY 106
A SPECIAL CELEBRATION 108
A WARM SEPTEMBER MORN 110
BEFORE THE STORM 112

Dedication

*To the family
And friends who had faith
In me and always encouraged
Me to reach for my dreams.*

INTRODUCTION

I wrote this book as a legacy, a gift to those I love and future generations. I anticipate that everyone who reads this book will be blessed in some way by the words God has given me.

God always obliges us. He makes a way out of no way and He always rewards our faithfulness. That's His promise to us. He shows us His faithfulness throughout the Bible and every day in our lives. In "Signs Of Faith", Chapter 1, you will see how faith is shown in different ways through people and especially through our Heavenly Father.

The "Sights And Sounds Of Life" many times helps us make it through another day. God's faithfulness is shone in each poem, particularly in the poems, "Thy Most Excellent Handiwork" and "An Early Spring." You'll see how some of the everyday sights and sounds can help us to be truly appreciative.

When God blesses our lives, many times it is through special people. He has sent many people into my life who have in particular been blessings to me, like my mother in "Beloved", and "Cicily Evangeline" and "Joseph Zacharia", my great niece and great nephew. My life has been greatly impacted by countless others who have left an impression in one way or another.

Events, whether they be good or bad can serve as reminders of how we can really know that God's hand is upon our lives. Many unfortunate incidences that have occurred, both by man's own hands and by nature, have brought us together and made us one. Often we come together as one to celebrate special occasions and to enjoy each other's company.

I trust you will enjoy reading these poems. Read them alone or with family or friends. Please enjoy them as much as I enjoyed writing them.

SIGNS OF FAITH

WHEN I PRAY

When I pray, I separate myself;
I go into my closet.
I know that what I pray for in righteousness,
My Father will not forget.

My morning prayer begins with
Honor to the Lord on high.
He does not sleep nor does He slumber,
But keeps a watchful eye.

I breathe a prayer with every breath
As I go throughout my day.
I lift those on my prayer list,
And others when I pray.

My faintest prayer reaches
My omnipotent Father's ears.
My flesh is weak but my spirit is willing.
It's His Spirit that hears.

When I repeat the words of the psalmist,
"Why art thou cast down, O my soul?"
He hears my crying voice,
And my heart He upholds.

In the evening, I thank my God
For the day that He has blessed.
I talk with Him awhile
Before I take my rest.

Sometimes I kneel before Him
With many praises, and I glorify my Lord.
Sometimes I just listen to Him speak
To my spirit, I do not say a word.

Oft times I lay before Him
With groans that would confuse man.
But, the Holy Spirit gives the utterance
That only God understands.

When I pray, it's just me and God;
A one-on-one conversation.
He extends the welcome,
And I gratefully accept the invitation.

BUT...

A little old lady needed more money
The other day in the grocery line.
But...I've had my eye on that new outfit
For such a long time.

I saw a homeless man walking
With an old canvas pack.
But...I was in traffic. I
Couldn't turn back.

There was a young mother
Watching her children at play.
She looked like she needed a friend.
But...it was none of my business anyway.

That sick person waited for a visit from
Some one who might care.
But...I couldn't do it today.
I didn't have a minute to spare.

There he sat in jail from
Committing a crime in haste.
He needed prayer and a word of hope.
But...its such a depressing place.

God saw us dying in sin,
Yet He did not turn away.
He sent us a Savior to
Die in our place one day.

He knew that Satan had come to
Destroy and utterly corrupt.
He sent Jesus to be the ultimate sacrifice.
What if Jesus had said, "But"?

DOWN AT THE WELL

Listen up, everybody.
I've got a story to tell.
About this man I met
Down at the well.

I sure was surprised when
He asked me for a drink, because you see,
He was a Jew, I'm a Samaritan.
He shouldn't have been talking to me.

Then He started telling me
All about my life
You know, about my five husbands
Each to whom I had been a wife.

He even told me of this man
I'm living with now,
Who isn't my husband.
Now how did He know that? How?

Everything this man told
Me was true. He was no liar.
This man must be a prophet....
I dare say He is. He's the Messiah.

He told me of this water
That would quench my thirst forever.
An eternal spring inside of me.
I never heard talk like this. No, never.

I'll telling you true, my neighbor,
If you want to change your life,
Come go with me down to the well.
Listen. Believe. For this is surely the Christ.

HOW MUCH?

Can't tell you how many
Stars are in the great big sky
Or how many grains of sand
The wind blew by.

Don't know the number
Of raindrops that fell today,
Or how many hairs
Are on my head. No, I just can't say.

Don't know why He lets
Us suffer trials and tribulations
But I do know He's there
through every situation.

And I do know who placed
The stars that glitter and glow
Down upon the sands
On the earth below.

The one God who made
The raindrops to fall
Is the same God who created
Everything both great and small.

Can't tell you how much
He loves me or even why,
But I can tell you I'll love
Him 'til the day I die.

I, EVE

Innocent like a new day
That never was before,
I ran through the garden,
Young, eager to explore.

I ruled with Adam over
Every living thing with dominion;
Over fish of the sea, fowl of the air,
And all other creation.

No loneliness knew Adam
For I was given to thee.
Nor did I know loneliness
With the mate given to me.

Hunger was as a stranger who
Found not a home with us.
Of nothing did we have need,
For nothing did we lust.

But then came the serpent;
Subtle darkness to deceive.
What manner of creature was this, hissing,
"Tis I you must believe"?

Was this a truth He spoke?
Would I know both evil and good
If I ate of the tree which
In the center of Eden stood?

I tasted of it's fruit and
It was surely good.
I gave also unto Adam,
For by my side He stood.

Then with eyes opened wide,
We knew the nakedness of the other.
'Twas then we plucked fig leaves
To hide us one from another.

The Father called to us as we hid
in the cool of the day.
He knew what we had done,
but wanted that we should say.

I, Eve, mother of all mankind
and every generation to come,
Knew shame as never before
when I saw this thing we had done.

But God loved us so much,
We being His very own;
Having breathed His breathe into Adam
And made me bone of his bone.

With overwhelming despair,
A troubled and burdened heart,
I labored for that which
Would bring forth a new start.

My redeemer would come one day
From my very own seed
To be a living sacrifice
For all my children; even I, Eve.

I GIVE YOU MY ALL

Father, there is praise for You
In my mouth every day.
If I could not speak,
It would still be the same way.

I'd clap out a tune that
Could be heard on high.
If I had no hands,
I would not ask you "why"?

My feet would shout out
The praise that is for You.
Without my feet, I would
Still give You what's due.

My eyes could see Your written word,
And read into my spirit
What You want to tell me,
Or maybe I could hear it.

My ears would listen to
What others have to say
About Your Son, Jesus,
And how He is "The Way".

You see, there is no reason
When we hear You call,
For us not to say,
"Truly, I give You my all".

MASTERPIECE

You are a masterpiece
A rare and precious art,
Created from the depths
Of the dear Master's Heart.

He lovingly shaped you,
Molded and formed.
He had a plan for you,
Even before you were born.

From the foundations of the Earth,
While in your mother's womb,
He planned out your life,
Even beyond the tomb.

You had to endure those trials
To get to where you are;
But He's not through yet.
You're destined to go far.

Among all of this world's goods,
You're an exclusive, precious stone;
A prized possession, a pearl,
Created by God alone.

So, lift up your head,
You marvelous and beautiful treasure.
When God made you,
He took great delight and pleasure.

And, though He designed
And fashioned you after Himself,
There's only one you;
You're a masterpiece, like nobody else.

THE BURDENS

Such a heavy load I felt
I was destined to endure.
The pain was unbearable,
Yet I was completely sure

If I could just get to the Master,
He would hear my case.
If only I could get to Him,
He would take my place.

He would lift my burdens
And bear them each Himself.
Why did I think I had to
Endure them all by myself?

I trudged down the road
Dragging the heavy weight.
Maybe He would not accept them.
Maybe I was too late.

I was so humiliated exposing
My shame to man,
But I had to let go and let God;
Like only He can.

Finally, I reached my destination,
I climbed the lofty stair.
I found the jury was waiting,
But Jesus met me there.

He took my case before the Judge
And they discussed my plight.
Jesus said, "She's mine, Father,
And I have made everything alright".

There's no condemnation in her,
All has been forgiven.
She has repented of her sins,
And the way she has been living.

Why had I carried that heavy
Load down every road and street?
For had I only asked, I could have
Laid them down at His feet.

UPON MOUNT CALVARY

I once stood upon a hill
One quiet, overcast day.
The leaves on the trees quivered
As a sudden breeze made them sway.

Could this have been like the hill
Upon which The Lord died for me?
The hill on which He gave His life;
The hill called Mount Calvary?

I thought I saw in the distance
A crowd slowly appearing.
They were approaching the hill,
And I saw, as they were nearing,

A man in the midst of the crowd
Bent down beneath a heavy burden.
The man...looked like Jesus!
Yes, I could see my Lord emerging!

I knew not what to do,
But as I turned to take flight,
I saw two crosses looming;
One on my left, one on my right.

No one seemed to notice me
As I stood there in awe.
Then, with blood mingled with
Sweat and tears, the Savior's face I saw.

As they nailed Him to the Cross,
Each stroke, I knew, was mine.
Each stripe He bore was the suffering
For the sins of all mankind.

I humbly bowed my head and I
Dropped down to my knees,
As they lifted Him up and hung Him high
Between the crosses of two thieves.

The others did not see me, but
The Savior saw and knew.
With arms outstretched, He looked down and said,
"This is how much I love you".

With tears in my eyes I looked around,
Yet, no one was there but me.
But, I'll never forget that day
I met my Savior upon Mount Calvary.

SOME DAYS, LORD

Some days are a struggle.
Some days there is strife and trouble.
Some days the cold winds blow
And I just don't know which way to go.

But I do know this one thing;
Whatever this life may bring,
Goodness and mercy shall be mine
When I place my hand in Thine.

And when I start to forget
By letting trifling things get me upset,
A silent prayer I breathe,
And You my fears relieve.

In You I find sweet peace;
For a higher mark I reach.
I'll labor to do your will.
I'll keep on until

One day in that heavenly place
I'll see Your shining face.
Then I'll know that it was all worthwhile
When I hear You say, "Rest now, my child".

ALL THAT MATTERS

My faith in You is all that
Matters when all is said and done.
This faith I have is all that matters
Though battles be lost or won.

Life's storms fiercely rage
And beat against my soul,
The effects of this world's anger and
Strife take their devastating toll

My faith in You is all that
Matters in spite of the works I do.
This faith I have is all that matters,
It's the only way to please You.

My faith in You is all that matters;
By faith I accepted salvation.
This faith I have is all that matters;
A sure and solid foundation.

I will have faith in You, for You
Hold my future in the palms of Your hands.
For Your will shall be done,
Even after I've said my final amen.

HEAVEN SENT

Oh, how my unrequited spirit
Longed for what my heart desired.
When would my heavenly Father
Bless me with what my soul required?

Is it also not good for woman,
As it is for man, to be alone?
Was I not also made from
The very bone of his bone?

Yet, I should not have questioned my
Heavenly Father's ways.
Be it His will, I would serve Him,
Alone, for the rest of my days.

I would work in the fields, for this
Is my God-given gift.
I would not dwell on my wants.
but, seek others to uplift.

Yet, while working in the fields
With other servants in one accord,
There, I met my Boaz, also
Working for The Lord.

We knew right away when
We set eyes on each other
That was the chosen time and place;
Heaven sent and planned by our Father.

Thus, He had not forgotten us.
He had always heard our prayers,
And kept us for each other,
In spite of all life's snares.

Now we shall serve Our God
All of the days of our lives, together.
We know that He will be with us
Through any kind of weather.

Continue ye also to wait upon the Lord,
Be virtuous, just, and obedient.
He will give you your heart's desire;
A blessing that is Heaven sent.

SANCTUARY

Peace envelopes my being.
My mind is suddenly renewed
With the truth of You.
My heart leaps; I am totally infused

With the reality of who I am
And the promise of who You are.
A quiet voice whispers
"We are not far apart."

Purify these chambers,
Make haste, do not tarry.
Come, live here, dwell within,
Make me a sanctuary.

Come right now, Holy Spirit;
Enter into my soul
Fill me with Your precious gifts;
All these walls can hold.

I humbly give myself
Lord, do what is necessary
To make me ready and willing
To be a sanctuary.

LAMENTATION

Life more abundantly;
That's what You said it would be.
That's what You
promised You came to give me.

I look for Your face
In so many places.
I seek Your face
Among so many faces.

What mistakes am I making?
I can't seem to find You.
Sometimes when I really need You,
I only feel sad, lonely and blue.

I look for You in the material things;
In situations, in people.
In things I do. Where are You?
I even seek you under steeples.

Why can't I seem to accomplish anything,
No one seems to even know or care
Whether I exist or not.
No one is there.

No matter how hard I try, all my
Efforts seem to be in vain.
I send You my heartfelt prayers.
I tell You my heart's pain.

My heart is breaking.
I feel it. I hear it shatter like glass
Against a cold stone floor.
I cry out in pain. Alas! Alas!

I pick up the pieces; assemble them carefully.
Lovingly I try to put the pieces together again
I handle it with the utmost care.
Wrapping it in cheap tape of cellophane.

If I don't, who will. You will. You will
Piece my heart back together.
Create a waterproof seal
Against any kind of weather

So even my tears won't dissolve the bond.
Even though life's flood may pour over my soul,
Please keep my heart from breaking again.
Please. Let the pieces hold.

CHAINS THAT BIND

Though you may joke
And curse as you please,
My friend, I tell you,
He still sees.

Though you may mock Him
And take His name in vain,
He still sees through to
The hurt and pain.

He can see down to
The depths of your soul,
Though your story
May have gone untold

To any mortal man
Near or wide.
From Him you cannot
Run away and hide.

From your sins, though scarlet
They may be,
Only an Almighty God
Can set you free.

Let Him break the
Chains that bind.
Let Him help you
Put the past behind.

No matter how lonely
And hurt you are,
Don't think that you
Have fallen too far.

For Him to reach way down
And lift you up,
Save your soul,
Then fill you up.

Put your life in
The safety of His hands.
Let Him lift you and
Help you stand.

On Christ the solid rock
You will stand.
It's all in
His master plan.

DAUGHTERS EMPOWERED TO POSSESS THE PROMISE

We are daughters empowered
To possess the promise.
The Word of the Lord
Is our assurance

That we've been given
The right by law
To walk into
Our inheritance.

As heirs of the promise,
We speak aloud,
And come to claim
That right.

With God on our side,
We can do all things,
For it's not by our power
Nor by our might.

Come forth, my sisters!
Realize your dreams.
Ye women so wise.
Just know this;

We have come together
As many voices.
We are daughters empowered
To possess the promise!

THE LOVE I OWE

I cried and I tried to
Forget the call from Him,
But the Holy Spirit shook me,
He overtook me, I let come Him in.

Thank God Almighty
For that glorious day
When I let the Son come
Into my life to stay.

Now brightly shines The Son
When the world outside grows dim.
Because of this marvelous light,
All my love is due Him.

I know I could never repay
The love I owe,
But I can love my neighbors
And let them know

That God works through me
To love them and show
This is how I can begin to
Give back the love I owe.

SON SHINE

The sun doesn't shine 'til
After the twilight's dark.
A baby must learn to crawl
Before he can stand up and walk.

The flowers cannot grow
Before ground-quenching rain.
We cannot gain true victory without
Trials and heart-wrenching pain.

Jesus endured merciless pain
While hanging upon the Cross.
Had He not suffered so,
We would be eternally lost.

God sent His only Son to
Show us the true way.
Now it is up to us to decide
How we live each day.

In the liberating shadow of the Cross
Or bound by darkness and sin,
Choose this day to open your
Heart and let the Son shine in.

MORNING JOY

Oh, what joy in the morning when I awaken
And first open my eyes.
I renew myself with the breath of life,
Then right away I realize,

He was there throughout the night,
Just like He said He would be.
The bright sunshine sends rays of light,
So clearly now I see.

The weeping I endured all night long;
The travailing and the pain;
The worrying and the frustration
Now all seemed to have been in vain.

The grass is greener, the sky looks bluer,
The flowers are brighter, too.
The air is fresher, the birds sings sweeter,
All because of You.

In the night times of my life
When I feel I can't go on,
You give me a new attitude
And fill my heart with song.

ENDLESS TALK

Sometimes in deep despair
I have shed quite a tear.
But, instead of listening to the destroyer of life,
I hear the destroyer of fear.

He knows what's inside of me.
He knows what makes me afraid.
But He says, "Be still My child.
Peace to you, I bade".

He says, "Come take my hand.
Let us take a walk.
Let us travel on this journey.
We'll have an endless talk".

He tells me how with Him
All things I can overcome;
How I can mount up with wings
Like eagles; be confident and strong.

He tells me not to fear for loved ones,
For they are in His care;
To continue to love them,
And lift them up in prayer.

He tells me to keep trusting in Him
As we continue to walk
On this life's journey
And have our endless talk.

REFINING FIRE

Refining fire,
Come, purify my soul.
Wash me, cleanse me,
Make me whole.

Shape me, stretch me,
Bend and mold.
Try me until I come
Out pure gold.

Refining fire,
Singe me to the core.
Let me know that
There's a need for more.

I'm going through pain
And hurt each and every day.
But I hear You saying
This is the only way.

This is the fire that
Purges and renews,
Making me an instrument
That can rightly be used

To do Your will with a
Pure and righteous heart,
And Your Word to
Rightly impart.

For a world whose thirst
For The Living Water is dire;
May my soul always feel
The heat of Thy refining fire.

GLITTERING HOPE

As I let my mind escape beyond
What I think I can achieve
To what I know God can do
Through me when I start to believe,

I am exhilarated; my soul
Soars on high,
For I know I have potential
Beyond my mind's eye.

There is a hesitation that
Comes over me sometimes
That makes me want to retreat
To a safeness behind.

Yet I release yesterday's no's
To embrace God's promises
As I turn toward tomorrow's hopes
And reassuring yeses.

I've heard of a truth…there is
No fear in the spirit He gave.
I've heard of His promise to be with me
As I trod the road He paved.

There's a light that shines a-bright
Like a diamond pure and rare.
The rays of glittering hope
Await the faithful who dare.

Jesus is that hope
Deep within my soul.
The reins of glittering hope
I now take hold.

Though the valleys may be low
And the mountains may be high,
It's not too much to believe that
I will one day touch the sky.

HE WAS ALWAYS THERE

When I thought that He was gone
And I felt so all alone
And the dark clouds hovered over my head,
I had just to go in prayer
And found He was always there
For it was I who wandered instead.

I knew He would never leave me,
Though sometimes it was hard to see
Because of this world and all of it's care.
But because of His love,
He spoke soft as a dove,
He whispered, "I was always there."

Whenever I would fear,
A still small voice I would hear,
And I knew it was His Holy Spirit.
It told me I could go on,
That I was not alone,
If only I could be still to hear it.

I looked for peace of mind,
And contentment I did find
When my burdens I laid down at His feet.
Now, regardless of the storm,
I'm free from all harm,
Because one day my Savior I will meet.

PRAISE!

Praise Him in good times
And all seems so right.
Praise Him when suddenly
Your daytime turns to night.

Praise Him when all is clear
And there is no sign of rain.
Praise Him when it pours nothing
But grief, trouble, and pain.

Praise Him when all your loved ones
Are gathered in one place.
Praise Him when even the sunshine
Seems to hide its face.

Praise Him with thy whole being.
Give Him the highest honor.
Let Him fill your life with blessings
And everlasting favor.

Glory hallelujah to
The Lord God Almighty!
For it's He who deserves the praise.
There is no other above Thee.

IF...

If....man could really do unto others
What he would have others do unto him,
Than there would be no need
To point fingers and condemn.

If....we could teach our children
To love and not to hate,
Maybe they could help change this world
Before it's too late.

If....we could sacrifice a few meals and
Give the money instead,
There would be food to make sure
Those who are hungry are fed.

If....we could see past the windows
Of our high ivory towers,
We would know that the world
Is not a bed of flowers.

If....we could go beyond the walls of the church
And from under the safety of the steeple,
We would see that there is a world
Full of forgotten lonely people.

If....we are all God's children and we
Have the same Heavenly Father,
Than why can't we love each other as brothers
And finally come together?

GO TELL THEM

Go shout it from the mountaintops!
In the valleys, let it be heard.
Proclaim Jesus is forever more.
The Everlasting Word.

Go ye into all the world,
From whence the four winds blow.
North, South, East, and West,
Let the populations know.

Go out into the hedges and highways.
Go tell them from coast to coast
That Jesus is the living Word
And He saves to the utmost.

With wings like eagles,
The weary can take flight.
Let the oppressed come by day
For soon cometh the night.

Though some may not believe.
Others will accept Him.
All must be told.
Now is the time. Go tell them.

IT'S ABOUT MY SAVIOR

It's not about me;
It's about my Savior.
It's not about me;
It's about Him.

In the frailty
Of my mortal flesh,
My chances continue
To be slim

That I could scarcely
Die in my own place
Or save my
Own sinful soul.

How could I
Put the broken
Pieces together
To make myself whole?

My Savior died
In my place.
He's given what no one
Else could ever give.

He gave me eternal life
Beyond this life
And promised forever
With Him I could live.

It's not about me or
The good works I've done,
Nor what I do now or
Forever more.

It's about what He did
Way back on Calvary;
It's not about me;
It's about my Savior

GUIDE MY STEPS

Guide my steps
Oh Lord I pray,
Lead me in
Thy precious way.

Let me seek
Thy will, no mine
And follow no other
Path but Thine.

Order my steps
By Your word.
May they be not ensnared
By sin, oh Lord.

As I turn my face
To the Son,
Guide my steps,
Lead me on.

Keep my feet
From the miry clay,
Guide my steps
Every day.

I AM A SERVANT

I am a servant of The Lord,
His eyes, His voice, His hands, His feet.
The eyes of God see through me
To everyone I meet.

I am His eyes so I can see
To the depths of others' pain,
Though they hide their broken hearts,
And whitened sepulcheres remain.

I am a servant of the Lord,
His eyes, His voice, His hands, His feet.
The voice of God speaks through me
To everyone I meet.

I am His voice because I speak
His truth to all with ears to hear.
Praise His name and lift Him high
To every man far and near.

I am a servant of The Lord,
His eyes, His voice, His hands, His feet.
The hands of God work through me
For everyone I meet.

I am His hands to touch and care
For others who are hurting.
To labor in the vineyard
'Til I take my rest from working.

I am a servant of the Lord
His eyes, His voice, His hands, His feet.
The feet of God walk with me
To everyone I meet.

I am His feet for I will
Go wherever He may send me;
Be it to the ends of the earth
To give all that is within me.

HEART OF GRATITUDE

Lord, I humbly lift my hands,
My soul pours out with pleasure.
A delight, a joy that surpasses
All other; a sentiment beyond all measure.

I give all in appreciation, for my
Heart is filled to overflowing.
I sing a joyful song of praise,
Full well knowing

That it is You I owe for
Every good thing that comes my way,
And for every single breath I take;
Every step into a new day.

Words cannot express
Everything I want to say;
Oh, how You always let me know
All will be okay.

I'm reminded of the wine pots
That never seemed to cease.
No matter what was poured out
There was always increase.

So goes my gratitude
For a God so faithful and just.
The God in whom
I will forever put my every trust.

THE VISITOR

One evening, a man had a visitor. The man was compelled to let the visitor come in and sup with him. After supper, the two sat and talked. The man began,
"I suppose you are wondering why I live out here all alone and so far away from others."
The visitor asked, "Why?"
The man explained. "I have been hurt so badly by family and friends, I don't want anything to do with them anymore. I wouldn't give them anything, even if I saw them dying." He had become very bitter over the years.
Then he asked the visitor, "Have you ever been hurt that badly by others?"
The visitor replied, "Yes, I have been hurt very badly."
Then the man said, "Could you give those who have hurt you so badly anything at all?"
The visitor again replied, "I did."
The man exclaimed loudly, "I hope you didn't give them anything of value!"
After a short pause, the man asked his visitor, "What in the world could you have given?"
The visitor replied, "I gave my life."
Immediately, the man realized his visitor was Jesus Christ.
Then, remorsefully, the man cried, "Lord, have mercy!"
Wiping the man's tears away, Jesus softly answered, "I did."

SIGHTS AND SOUNDS OF LIFE

THY MOST EXCELLENT HANDIWORK

Oh, how Thy excellent handiwork
Extols the glory of Thy presence!
The sea whirls and twirls and splashes
In a clash of effervescence.

White lightning flashes
And rolling thunder claps.
Surely these awesome wonders
Could not perchance be mishaps.

The sun beaming in it's gold-ness
Shines down from a sky of vast blue
Til the moon comes out to hang around
In velvet twilight hue.

The silvery stars twinkle
In random applaud.
As they, too, give thanks
To an Almighty God.

The Earth yields forth lush vegetation
For our sustenance each day.
Flowers burst forth in a rainbow of colors;
What a glorious display!

The trees resound with the sounds
Of sparrows' delightful trills.
And I, too, lift my voice to sing hallelujah
As I lift my eyes to the hills.

Then I lift my eyes just a little bit higher
To the heavens up above.
I say "Thank You, Lord, for Your mercy
And sacrificial love.

Thank You, Lord, for saving me
When I was about to fall.
Now I know that I am, by grace,
Thy Most Excellent Handiwork of all.

MY HEART'S SONG

My heart's song is the tempo of my life's
Blood beating through my veins
Telling me lest I doubt, "He lives! He lives!
He still reigns!"

It is the sound of a joyful chorus singing
With a sweet lilt and a swaying melody
That sends a rhythm through my soul
Whenever I think of Thee.

My heart's song is a delight that makes me
Want to run and shout it to everyone
That God loved me so much, *me*, that
He sent His only begotten Son.

My heart's song is a gift from my Savior
That lets me ask what can I give in return
For a love so unconditional, so real, so true;
A love I did not have to earn.

My heart's song is an everlasting note
In a symphony of symphonies
Lead by the Maestro of all
The choirs in the heaven-lies.

My heart sings as He composes
A masterpiece in me
And lets my heart's song go
On forever and ever throughout eternity.

ALL IN A DAY'S WORK

My alarm blasts,
Time to rise.
I jump out of bed,
Lazily wiping sleep from my eyes.

Whispering a hasty prayer
Beneath my breath,
I mindlessly brush my teeth
And run a quick bath.

I rummage for my clothes,
No time to poke around;
Just enough time to
Swallow a cup of coffee down.

With a bound out the door,
I finally get on the road.
While fighting the morning traffic,
I think about my day's workload.

I rush in to work
And throw myself into my daily tasks.
Finally! With an exhausted sigh,
It's time to go at last!

Weaving my way through
The traffic lights,
I wonder, "What's for
Dinner tonight?"

To late to cook;
Time just flies.
I'll just pick up
Some burgers and some fries.

Content with my day's work,
I lie in bed calm and collected.
Then, I suddenly remember
Something I have sadly neglected.

I haven't taken the time
Out of my busy day's chores
To properly acknowledge and praise
The works of the Lord

Who perfectly formed the earth,
The sky and the sea,
And all in a day's work He
Lovingly created me.

I AM HIS WOMAN

I am His woman.
I am made in His image.
I am black like the nights of my native land.
I am white like ivory. I am red like the clay of the earth.
I am yellow like the oriental sun.

I am His woman.

I am different from my sister.
I walk different from my sister.
I talk different from my sister.
I look different from my sister.
I am the fairest of the fair to look upon.
I am uncomely in outward appearance.
Yet I am the apple of His eye.

I am His woman.

I am broad with full arms to
embrace the ones I love.
I am slight, but sturdy like the mighty oak.
I am a young woman with
hope of new life before me.
I am a grandmother with years of wisdom
to give to my children and their children;
a legacy for the generations to come.

I am His woman.

I have been sheltered from the
adversities that have come my way.
I have been tossed and battered
by the storms of life.
Still, I have trusted and endured.

I am His woman.

I live in a big city where the sights
and sounds and people are fast.
I live in a country town where
there is time to smell the roses.
I live in a thatched hut in an African village.
I live in a stately mansion on a hill.
I am His woman.

I am the innocence of Eve.
I am the loyalty of Ruth.
I am the blessedness of Mary.
I am the royalty of Esther.

I am His woman.

I am a woman of a powerful spirit.
I am a woman of a steel strength.
I am a woman of an unwavering faith.
I am a woman of God.
For He is my God.

And I am His woman.

OLD MAN WINTER

Old Man Winter, sluggish in breath,
Unhurried from his slumber,
Sending gentle puffs of air, a
Warning to no avail, of his wrath.
Quickly, surely, strength returns.
The forecast: Longevity and endurance
For the Length of his days.
A blast of wind exploding
From the very depths
Of the old man's being
Freezing the innermost
Parts of all mankind.
Chilling hands, hearts, some
Souls, forever; like a vice
With it's relentless grasp.
Though like an eternity, yet
by and by, his bony, iron-like
Grip is released. His strength
Wanes, giving way to healing.
Old man, lie down. Spring awaits
To be birthed and to suckle at
Mother Earth's breasts.

AN EARLY SPRING

Waters trickling down
From snow-capped peaks
Meeting with bodies
Of cool mountain creeks,

Brimming with vibrant
New aquatic life
While Spring announces
That she has arrived.

An early Spring has
Just been born
To Mother Earth's pride
And Winter's scorn.

To life that has lain
Dormant for ages
Between the leaves
Of unturned pages.

Gentle, warm breezes
Send fragrant perfume
Throughout the air
from flowers in bloom.

Light, soft rains
Cover the fields
To bring in bountiful
Autumn yields.

A sparrow serenades
Humanity from the crest
Of a lofty oak tree
Which houses her nest.

Squirrels scamper around
With watchful eyes
Gathering food to replenish
Next winter's supplies.

The earth is fresh and green.
The cobwebs are swept away.
New love is born, old love rekindles.
Hearts are light and gay.

Winter does not last forever,
Cold does not for eternity cling.
God's way of reminding us;
He sends us an early spring.

ANOTHER EASTER SUNDAY MORNING

It's another Easter Sunday morning
And bells are ringing through the air.
The birds are singing their sweet refrains,
As if to say, "Rest, now, from your care".

Time to join with other worshippers;
Time to sing and lift our voices.
Time to shout out, "Hallelujah!"
And join with the choir in chorus.

A joyful noise fills the church as neighbor
Greets neighbor with a "good day".
A sweet presence is felt all over the place
As heads are bowed to pray.

We honor The Lord on this day
Who sacrificed His life upon the cross
That we all would repent from our sins;
Be saved and draw the lost.

Hearty Amen's are shouted from among
The faithful in the congregation.
The preacher continues to heat things up
With an inspiring sermon on salvation.

After the service, families are gathered
For dinner and thanks to The Great "I am".
It's not just on Easter Sunday, but everyday
That we remember the sacrificial lamb.

THE SUMMERS OF OUR YOUTH

It's the early gray part of the morning
When movements anywhere are few
And heavy quiet hangs over a land
That's spread with a sheet of misty dew.

Slowly, I awake from a good night's sleep,
I arise, step foot on the floor.
Then, I make my way through the house
And I stick my head out the door.

The grayness of the morning is just about gone
As an orange sun arises in the east.
I step out onto the porch and hear chirping and peeps
As the early birds make worms their feast.

The sun's brightness shines down as it sparkles
And shimmers through the trees.
It's rays beam through as they gently
Embrace and caress all the leaves.

My mind goes back many years ago to a time
When I was young and carefree;
To a world that seemed so bright and sunny
And all of life was before me.

We would get up, bathe and eat,
All before the crack of dawn.
Then, be outside before you knew it,
Cutting somersaults on the grassy lawn.

We would play so hard and get so tired,
Then go inside for water.
Our parents would see us all dusty and dirty
And call us their "little dirt daubers."

By noon, the heavens were like a clear, blue sea
With fluffy white ships sailing by.
We'd lie on our backs upon the grass
And dream as we gazed upon the sky.

Then Mama called us in to eat lunch
Before going back out
To play hide and seek, tag, or
Ride our bikes about.

Then maybe we would rest in
A quiet and shady spot
Or dip our feet in a cool stream;
That felt good when it was hot.

At dinnertime, everyone sat to eat.
Were we hungry after playing so hard!
Then everyone would go outside;
Mama and Daddy on the porch;
Us kids in the yard.

We stayed outside 'til almost dark
And mosquitoes came out to bite.
We knew it was time to go inside
When lightening bugs started to light.

We took out baths and said our prayers
And jumped into our beds
When dreams of a day in the summers of our youth
Paraded through our heads.

SPECIAL PEOPLE

BELOVED

She touched each and every one who
Ever came into contact with her.
Her smile so sweet, her haughty laugh
Left an impression on all there-after.

Her faithfulness to her God and family
Was one thing that made her so dear.
Showing others by her caring ways
Was her purpose for being here.

She raised her children with a gentle hand,
Teaching them by God's Holy rules;
With a loving hand she taught them
To be tall and strong in this world so cruel.

She was the perfect example of a mother
Whose children would grow up to call her blessed.
Others admired her strength, though there
Were many times she was tried and tested.

She was dearly adored as a
Daughter, sister, mother, and wife.
She filled each role lovingly
Each and every day of her life.

I know she's leading the angels in song now
And worshiping her Lord up above,
Memories of her will live on and on,
For she will always be our beloved.

THE CALLING

When you first met the Lord
And excepted your salvation,
You gave Him your life
With unwavering dedication.

But surely you never imagined
Or dared to even dream
The plan He had for you
In His awesome scheme.

He took you and He lead you
And you let Him have His way.
He said, "I want to use you
To guide My sheep today".

Having girded your loins
And put your hands to the plow,
Armed with your vision,
There was no turning back now.

You knew it wouldn't be easy
After you heard "the call",
But you knew you had to tell
Others before the fall

About someone who loved them so
He was crucified for them,
So they could have eternal life
And live forever with Him.

You had to tell them of a Savior
Who would forgive their every sin.
You had to tell them how to accept
Salvation and someday enter in.

You had to tell how God
Wants them to witness to others.
And how those others should
Tell their sisters and brothers.

Then we will all stand before the King,
God's only Begotten Son.
You will know your work was not in vain
When you hear Him say, "Well done".

TRIBUTE TO A SPECIAL LADY

A friend, a businesswoman,
A wife, and a mom,
You may seem to be tireless
In the eyes of some.

But since God has called you,
And equipped you for His plan;
Blessed you with wonderful children,
And a God-fearing man,

You can rest assured
He will carry you through.
He will help you to do
All you need to do.

The life that you lead
And the lives that you touch
Are what make you extra-special.
That's why we love you so much.

Your children love you
And tell you you're alright.
You're number one mom
In their sights.

Your husband loves you
And aside from Jesus Christ,
Tells you that you are
First, lady, in his life.

With God, all things are possible.
You have shown this to be true.
You deserve this special tribute
Dedicated to you.

When the going gets tough,
You know it's just a test.
Among special ladies,
You are one of the best.

A RARE JEWEL

You have basked in the sunshine.
You have weathered the storm.
You have walked hand in hand with God,
Who has kept you from great harm.

Yes, you have been dealt some blows.
Some mountains were placed in your way.
And I know at times you have been
Down-hearted, but I just have to say,

I have seen but few
With a more faithful spirit.
When some said you could not make it,
You just would not hear it.

You knew that He was on your side
And "from whence cometh your help".
Because He said it, you believed it.
On His word you trusted
And vowed to accept.

You have always given to others, though
At times you have had so little to give them.
But your little became much, for in
God's eyes, you did it for Him.

A loving smile that beams so bright,
Others find comfort in it's radiance.
A caring nature that has endeared you
To all who have come into your presence.

You are that beautiful, rare jewel
That others cannot seem to find.
But I am blessed to know you,
For you are truly one of a kind.

TO MY SISTER

I just want you to know
Just how much I care.
Love is the tie that binds
And the mighty bond we share.

Through the years our heartfelt
Words have often gone unspoken.
I want you to know that
Bond of love will never be unbroken.

You were always the feisty one,
You never gave up on a fight.
You were the one who was always there
To make sure things were right.

You sometimes amazed me,
You were always willing to learn.
I admired the way you spoke your mind,
You were always strong and stern.

What a wonderful quality you have
Of being concerned for all.
You give to others whatever the need;
Whether it's great or small.

You probably think you see the stains
Of teardrops on these pages.
But the stains are from tears of joy
Of our lives down through the ages.

These are just a few words from within
To show my gratitude and love.
My dear sister you're a blessing,
Sent from our Father above.

SISTERS IN CHRIST

I asked the Lord to send someone
In whom I could trust;
A real friend who would be
Honest and just.

When I met you, I knew He
Had answered my prayer.
You're my sister-in-Christ,
With whom I have much to share.

We have Jesus in common,
And to us that's enough.
He's right in the midst,
Even when the going gets tough.

We have a friendship
That's loving and true.
Blessed by our Father
Through and through.

We've treasured the good times
And we've endured the bad.
We've laughed through the happy times
And we've cried through the sad.

You know my weaknesses
And I know your strengths.
We know for each other
We would go to great lengths.

And when I'm blue and
Feeling kind of low,
I don't need to say a word;
You just seem to know.

The day can be gray
With dark clouds looming.
Just a call from you, friend,
And it seems like flowers are blooming.

When we start sharing,
Our problems seem but few.
When we pray together,
Our troubles melt like dew.

Your friendship is like the sun
Shining in my heart.
I pray that wherever we go in life,
We're never too far apart

To call on each other
And lift each other up.
May God abundantly bless your life
And truly fill your cup.

CICILY EVANGELINE

Cicily Evangeline, little girl child;
Soft and sweet, gentle and mild.
It's about time you came out
To see what this old world is all about.

You've arrived from your resting place;
You've opened your innocent eyes.
All things will be a wonder;
Each day a new surprise.

You'll play with your dolls
In your little-girl world,
And wear ribbons in your
head full of braids and curls.

You're here for a reason,
There's a plan for your life.
But, God knew when He created you
All would not be sunny and bright.

With a wisdom of the ages
Echoing through all of time,
There's a truth of a love that leads
With a Holy power divine.

With gentle hands to teach you
And loving hands to chasten you,
His presence will be there to protect
And take you all the way through.

Cicily Evangeline, little girl child,
When you take Jesus as your guide,
Your resting place will be in Him
And in His care you will abide.

JOSEPH ZACHARIA

You're a blessed little boy,
Joseph Zacharia.
With wings like an eagle,
soar, fly higher.

With Jesus as the wind
beneath your wings,
You can be sure
you can do all things.

As you go through life,
you may travel some miles
Through the valley of despair,
and suffer some trials.

But talk to Jesus
every day in prayer.
He will always be with you
if you meet Him there.

He will give you peace
and unspeakable joy.
Because today
you're our little boy,

But tomorrow you
will be a grown man,
Walk all the way with
your hand in Jesus' hand.

This is my prayer for you,
Joseph Zacharia.
That you spread your wings,
soar, fly higher.

THAT'S WHY I CALL YOU FRIEND

It was when I wanted to be alone;
That's when I knew you cared.
You waited for me to get over it,
Then, oh, the talks we shared.

My life has been enriched
With a gift that money cannot buy.
For when I would have given up,
You said, "Don't. Just give it one more try".

Whenever I needed an ear to bend
Or a strong shoulder to cry on,
I knew you were near to lend
A helping hand; a friend I could rely on.

Sure, many believe in angels unseen;
I must confess, I do too.
But I also believe in angels we see,
Like the angel I see in you.

Shoulder to shoulder; back to back;
We're a force against the wind.
Your friendship has been strength in my life.
That's why I call you friend.

TRUE FRIENDSHIPS

True friendships are destined by God,
We cherish and savor each passing year.
The memories we store deep in our hearts,
As each one becomes more precious and dear.

Good friends are to be treasured above all
Things, like rare and priceless jewels.
Those who forsake true friendships
Should be counted among this world's fools.

Just as a bouquet of God's colorful flowers
No painter's palette can match,
The love that shines in a true friend's heart
No photographer's lens can catch.

True friendships work both ways
To build a bond that's sure.
And no matter how time changes us,
True friendships will remain secure.

STEPPING OUT

As you step into a new level in life
You wonder why you were chosen;
Why you were given the opportunity
To learn and to grow in.

Yet, nothing happens just to happen;
All things come about for a reason.
Perhaps it is now the moment in time
To come into your season.

You knew that in this great wide world
There had to be much more.
But, to get beyond those four walls,
You had to step through that door.

Go for it, reach higher and higher,
And I sincerely wish you well.
For I know that one day your testimony
Will be an awesome story to tell.

WHAT IS A NEIGHBOR?

A neighbor is he who lends
A helping hand and sends
Best regards to another,
A cheerful hello to a brother;
Goes out of the way to be friends.

A neighbor is he who gives a smile,
Or lingers to chat awhile
About issues of the day;
Maybe discuss a better way,
And offers help through a trial.

A neighbor is he who cares,
One who always shares
Whatever he may have,
If it will help pave
A way through some of life's snares.

A neighbor is he you'll find
May need a hand sometimes;
He who may be in need
Of a thoughtful, selfless deed
From one who's caring and kind

A neighbor can be right next door
Or someone you've never met before.
If the call comes for help,
Forget about yourself.
That's what neighbors are for.

ONE MAN STANDS UP

One man stood up
After being tempted for forty days.
To show us how we could resist
Satan and his evil, destructive ways.

One man stood up
After being called by God
To lead a nation to freedom
With just a simple rod.

One man stood up
Over forty years past
When he said "God will let us see
The promised land at last"!

He spoke of how all God's children,
Both black and white
Would one day hold hands;
Cease to kill each other and fight.

One man stood up when
He spoke of the possibility
Of our nation having an African American
President in thirty years, maybe forty.

One man stands up, as that vision comes to pass,
To lead millions of people to receive
The dream that all things are possible
If we only work together and believe.

MEMORABLE TIMES
AND EVENTS

AN ATTITUDE OF THANKSGIVING

It's Thanksgiving day, the family is here,
It's good to be gathered together.
It's cool and crisp outside;
The fall kind of weather.

The smells of roasting turkey and
Pumpkin pie are in the air.
Everybody's ready to sample
The delicious fare.

On television there are football games
With favorite teams at play.
And parades with marching bands
And floats with themes for the day.

Everyone's catching up on family news
And reminiscing about the past,
When finally comes the call to dinner.
Time to eat at last!

After everyone is seated and
We've finished laying out the spread,
We ask that we all join hands
And then we bow our heads.

We thank You, God, for who You are
In all of Your glory;
Because You are Lord,
We humbly bow before You.

We thank You for allowing us
To gather one more year.
We ask Your blessings upon those
Who could not be here.

We ask You to bless those who have
Lost loved ones dear to their hearts.
May they find peace in You,
And let the healing start.

Guide the leaders of our Nation.
Let each decision be the right choice.
Let them tune in to You
And hear only Your voice.

Bless those who hunger
And don't have enough to eat.
Bless those who don't have a
Warm floor on which to set their feet.

Humble our hearts; open our hands;
Grant us a giving spirit.
Thank You for blessing us with
More than enough that we may share it.

Thank You for letting us know
That we can always come to You
With "An attitude of Thanksgiving"
Now and the whole year through.

ONE HOLY NIGHT IN BETHLEHEM

One holy night in Bethlehem,
Over two thousand years ago,
A tremendous star shone in the eastern sky
Casing a very bright glow.

A star with a tail that pierced the night sky
Shined down to where Jesus lay,
In a lowly manger on a bed
That was carefully lined with hay.

The animals stood attentively as
They gazed at this wondrous sight
As if they knew somehow
The special-ness of this night.

An angel appeared to shepherds
In a field tending to their flock.
They were so struck with awe
And wonder that they could not talk.

The angel told them to arise and leave
To go see the newborn King;
And so they arose to follow, for honor
And praises they would bring.

They came to bow down before the cradle
To worship the newborn Savior
Who had come to save God's people
And change the world forever.

The wise men sent from
Herod traveled from afar
To find the child that was really King
And for whom shone the star.

The Magi came before the King
And knelt on bended knee;
And praised and worshipped Him
And offered their gifts to Thee.

They presented to Him gifts of
Frankincense and myrrh and gold
Which were gifts fit for a king
So it was told.

Being warned not to return to tell Herod
Where baby Jesus lay,
The wise men turned to travel on by
Going another way.

Mary and Joseph were so blessed
To have Jesus for a son,
But though they were His earthly parents
They knew He was The Chosen One.

Now, December twenty-fifth is
Much celebrated and we call it Christmas Day,
A time we decorate trees and give gifts
And are festive and gay.

But the real reason we call it
Christmas and joyously sing
Is because one holy night many years ago
God sent us the King of Kings.

GLAD TIDINGS

It's Christmas time and hurried
Shoppers rush to and fro,
Looking for sparkling tinsel, like
Silver with a radiant glow.

We need the perfect Christmas tree,
The tallest and greenest by far.
We must have decorations of red and
Gold and a big bright star.

There's bright wrappings and colored ribbons
To buy and Christmas cards to send.
We should prepare for visits from the folks.
And, oh, the parties to attend.

A colorful tie for Father;
A lovely silk scarf for mother, too;
A sweater for Uncle Ben
And a golden pin for Aunt Sue.

How about A doll for Sissy, and
That Video Game for Johnny.
No matter the cost, after all,
It is only money.

It seems like somewhere amidst
The hustle and bustle of the season,
That we all have forgotten the
Holiday's real reason.

Jesus the Christ was born many years
Ago into this sinful place
To die, to rise again and to save
Us all by His grace.

He showed us all by His life
How we should treat each other.
While we are feasting with our families,
Let us remember our less fortunate brother.

Why not give from our hearts to make
Someone else's life brighter?
Bless others with our best
Gifts to help make their load lighter.

While we worship with our families
And celebrate the birth of The King,
May we send glad tidings of great joy
While the Heavens and all the Earth sing.

WHILE ON THE CROSS THAT DAY

I adore Thee so much,
how much I cannot say.
For mere words cannot express
my feelings in any way.

The cross on which You hung
and the blood that You shed
The crown made of thorns
that was thrust upon Your head,

Are all signs of the passion
You spared not for me.
So wondrous was Your love,
how could I not see.

So amazing was Your faithfulness that
as Your eyes grew dim,
You looked down on those
who cried, "Crucify Him!"

They looked back and shouted
more angry words at You.
But You said, "Father forgive them,
for they know not what they do."

You bore all my sins while
on the cross that day.
You showed Satan he
would not have his way.

The day was overcast with
dark clouds and gloom
As they took You and laid You
into a borrowed tomb.

But early on that third day when
Mary came to see,
She found the stone rolled away;
the tomb was empty.

As Mary left in tears,
someone called to her.
Turning to see Jesus, she cried,
"Rabboni!" meaning Master.

Even old death had to
stand back and obey
As You rose from the grave
and conquered all that day.

So great a love for one
so unworthy as I.
You were obedient to the Father
to hang, bleed, and die.

Now You sit upon the throne
at the Father's right hand
Waiting one day to tell me
all I don't understand.

Even though I say I love You
and tell You every day,
I know You loved me more
while on the cross that day.

A SPECIAL CELEBRATION

It's a special celebration,
A happy and joyous event
To tell you when we said we
Loved you, exactly what we meant.

You were there throughout the years
You were right by our sides.
You were there in the good times,
And you took the bad times in stride.

You cooked, cleaned and washed
And nurtured wounds, too.
You were always there for us.
You were faithful and true.

You gave up a lot to make sure
we had what we needed.
You went out of your way,
And your goals you exceeded.

Raising small children wasn't
An easy task for a young mother,
But you did it, and we turned out great,
Because you're one like no other.

Now, there's a new generation;
The grands have now come along.
Mama is there to embrace them, too.
Of course, they can do no wrong.

You have endeared yourself to all
Who have really come to know you.
Many are here today to tell you that
And to honor you, too.

God has truly blessed you with a
Wonderful family that loves you so much.
To see how much we care
A heart can't help but be touched.

Families usually gather on birthdays,
holidays, and every other occasion.
But, at the center of this special gathering
Is you. It's a special celebration!

*A WARM SEPTEMBER MORN

It was a warm September morn.
There was a still, quiet calm.
When somewhere from out of the blue
There came great harm.

From out of the sky they
Hit without warning;
Throwing a world into shock,
Then into deep mourning.

Rachel wept as
The children died.
And our nation's faith
Was ultimately tried.

Whether they were there
Or whether far away,
No one's heart was
Left untouched that day.

But with a united voice,
We loudly proclaim
"The United States
Will rise again!"

United we stand,
Divided we fall.
Not for just a few;
It takes us all.

This country declares
"God is by our side,
And under God's shadow
We shall abide."

From somewhere among the rubble,
"Old Glory" stood proud and free.
Triumphantly waving her colors
For the whole world to see.

Thousands of innocent people
Lost their lives for naught.
But in the midst of tragedy,
Some valuable lessons were taught.

We learned to pray together,
Crossing the boundaries of church and state.
We learned to put aside our differences,
Our prejudices, our hate.

The tears will dry, the wounds will heal,
A stronger bond will form
Among those who remember,
For no one will forget that warm September morn.

*REMEMBERING SEPTEMBER 11, 2001 (911)

*BEFORE THE STORM

To those who think they lost
everything they had,
before the storm came one day
dark and sad
bringing destruction
and unthinkable spoil.
To those who stare
out of borrowed windows to
gaze upon the native soil
upon which once rested childhood homes.
To those who sat in lonely rooms
hoping someday they could
reach out of the gloom.
Not to scorn time's fateful hands,
but to pray and work together for
restoration of their land.
To those who look for reasons
why some were set apart.
This is the time to realize a brand new start;
a time to arise.
Arise my sister!
Arise my brother!
from the ashes of the past
to the resounding echoes that
cry, "Free at last! Free at last"!
To those who are among the
blessed number who came
through the flood
and out of the fire

with the power to stand tall and
rise up higher.
To those who have more than they
have really ever known
even before they think they lost
everything they had
Before the storm
came one day dark and sad.

*REMEMBERING HURRICANE KATRINA